W9-AQB-387

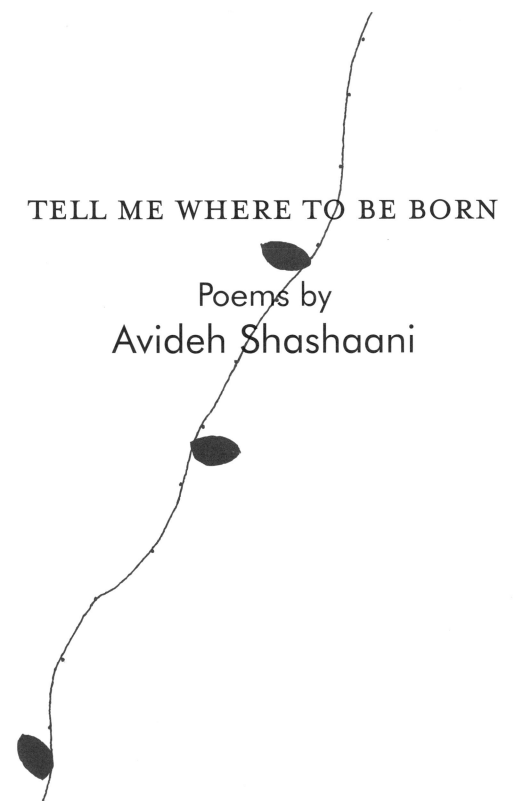

TELL ME WHERE TO BE BORN

Poems by
Avideh Shashaani

Forest Woods Media Productions Inc.
The Bunny and Crocodile Press
Washington, D.C.

For information please contact:

Fund for the Future of the Children
5101 Wisconsin Avenue, NW
Suite 230
Washington DC 20016
Telephone: 202-364-2606
Email: ffc@futureofchildren.net
Web address: http://www.futureofchildren.net

Cover design and typography by Sepi Alavi
Front cover photograph by Pablo Wilson
Back cover photograph by Connie Reider
Offset printing by Printing Press, Inc.

Library of Congress Control Number: 2008921432

ISBN: 9780938572442

First Edition 2008
Printed in the U.S.A.

In memory of Dorothy Devers

CONTENTS

ACKNOWLEDGMENTS

For their encouragement and unbounded generosity, I would like to thank Grace Cavalieri, Gordon and Mary Cosby, Marian Wright Edelman, and Ken McNeil.

I consider visionary and selfless philanthropy as a form of sacred art. My good friends Josephine Ammerman and Andrew Ammerman have taken this art form to its highest level. I would like to express my thanks to them for their long-standing support of our work on behalf of children and youth. Ambassador Helmut Tuerk and his wife Monika Tuerk have also been instrumental in nurturing the vision of our work at the Fund for the Future of our Children. To them I extend my heartfelt thanks as well.

I would like to thank my editor, Cynthia Rausch Allar; Sepi Alavi for taking the time from writing her thesis to typeset and design this book; Heather Bause and Jesse Webb for stepping in and providing last minute help. Grateful acknowledgment to the following for featuring some of these poems:

Asian American Female Poets Anthology (Deep Bowl Press), Bayeux Arts, Inc., Beltway Poetry Quarterly (online), Burma American Fund (online, Conference of Catholic Bishops (bookmark), Only the Sea Keeps: Poetry of the Tsunami (online), Forest Woods Media Productions, Poets for Darfur (online), and "The Poet and the Poem from the Library of Congress," public radio broadcast.

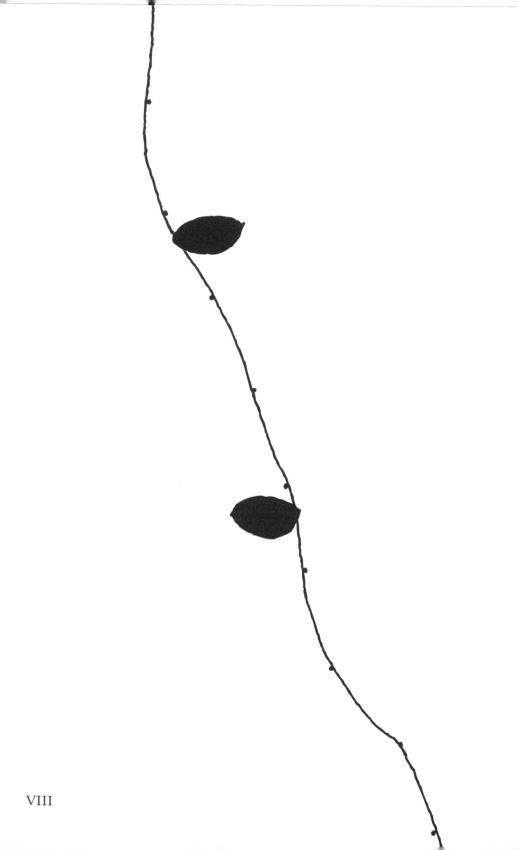

VIII

FOREWORD

Tell Me Where To Be Born is Avideh Shashaani's third book of
poems. It presents a challenge to the highest spirit in us. It asks
that our full attention be turned to the children of the world, with
the hope and knowledge that innocence is not a point of departure,
but a path of return.

How do we appraise these poems, since poetry is an incidence
of language? Do we look at the word choice? How do we
evaluate what a dream is worth? How can literary critics judge the
mythology of tenderness? Is the poet's world the only true world
there is? Should we trust it as reality?

All poetry is a balance of faith. The writer wonders: Will the reader
understand the intent? Often thoughts seem irrational to the mind,
yet are truly rational to the spirit of the poet, for poetry is ultimately
an argument against what is suppressed in society. It reports to the
world what is important to humankind.

In the title poem of the book, the author uses the child's point of
view, asking

…
tell me where to be born
so you will not hate me one day,
so you will not maim me one day,
so you will not kill me one day.
…

And here we have the underpinning of the entire book. Although
eloquence does not change sorrow, language can change grief to
vision, which is what I think the poet does here. I especially like the
poem "Wall of Innocence," where author writes:

…
The wild poppies covering

the hills with their scarlet hue
speak of a concealed dream
that lay bare beneath the sun.

These poems are easily seen as influenced by the mystical remembrances of Rumi and other spiritual antecedents who wrote with an unshakable faith in charity. If we say these writings are from an overriding emotion, then the Persian influence is obviously seen; if we look at the expression, the French poets come to mind— Valery, Baudelaire—and if we wish to describe the themes, then abandonment and death are present in all their intensities. We see the poet entering the landscape in "Baptism Pool:"

As the days go by
and the nights close in
my heart becomes
a baptism pool
from the plaintive tears
of the children lost to war.

When I am with other poets, I always ask, "What is your book about?" I guess I want to check my own responses. In fact, I often wonder about the reason why one poet will write of pain while another is chastened into silence by its power. In the background of each poem here, there is always the dwindling light of the poet's own childhood. Poetic technique and revelation are present in the line, but fueled most of all by empathy.

The poems in *Tell Me Where To Be Born* are tiny rituals of spirit and tone. They come from the "irrational" mind. The mission of poetic engagement is the subject matter. This is the "rational" world. The result of the book in total is one long glorious hymn. It is one we can rely on to make a difference.

So we turn to ask *who is this poet?* I have known Avideh for 25 years as a friend and fellow writer. Avideh Shashaani was born in Tehran and came to Washington, DC as a child where her father served as military and air attaché. She has dedicated her life to spiritual devotion. She received her Ph.D. in Sufi studies and has translated 10 mystical books from Persian to English, poems that would otherwise never have been seen in our language. The first part of her professional life was dedicated to working for the handicapped, serving in many capacities, including co-director for the United Nations Institute for Rehabilitation in Developing Countries. I've watched her surrender her personal time to organize "bridges" from country to country, bridges of voice across which children could walk and meet. I have seen her bring Palestinian children to talk to Israeli children in groundbreaking dialogue. Their artworks have been displayed as part of the dialogue in Washington DC.

This international city has served well as the locus for these operations. Not limited by geography, Avideh has created an international website that mentors and heals. Having founded the **Fund for the Future of Children**, Avideh reached to academic and religious leaders to illuminate her cause, to make it a cause for all of us, to help the children. Believing is seeing, and I have seen Avideh Shashaani host events at Georgetown University, George Washington University, and The French Embassy Theatre, among other cultural centers in our nation's capital. She has entered other institutions to galvanize energy if she believed they had found too little time to herald the children of the world.

When I met Avideh, I was assistant director for Children's Programming at corporate PBS. We immediately meshed. I knew above all others how financial funding came to children's programming last, if at all. Avideh was fighting a similar battle on another front. The emphasis was the same in many ways. We asked why children were always seen as the least of our citizens. What Avideh does in the world feels a lot like love. It feels as if she would prevent global death of children if she could, and what she does is to serve the lives of those who can be saved.

Shashaani's work with conferences, seminars, assemblies is dynamic. It is fascinating, yet its goal is not entertainment. Neither is that the goal of these poems. Journalistic writing for an audience is like gathering people together for an exchange of opinions. Poems are forms that do not invite exchange but beg engagement.

Poetry of Witness is also called Poetry of Purpose. It is a literary complaint that harks back to the earliest soldiers and the earliest wars. Most recently Latin America has given us the best poems of evocation. The American Carolyn Forche is best known to us recently as a poet of witness. We could not name many outstanding voices in the early part of the 20th century. Then the Cultural Revolution of the 1960's and the outrages of Vietnam made thousands of poets turn to political themes—injustice, racism, war, inequities, intolerance— addressing the political dynamic of the time. Yet, very few have addressed children, and no one has dedicated an entire book to the subject that I recall.

These words are from the poem "Child Soldier:"

...your soul left long ago
when humans used innocence
to murder for their cause.

There are poems in this world, certainly Avideh's among them, that assess global conditions whether assessment is fashionable or not. When we see visuals on TV, children in need of food and shelter, the sights are effective methods to get our attention. These same stories have been transformed into the sound that comes from a heart into poetry. Her impulse is to attend to needs as she sees them, hoping to interest us in those needs, in the name of children. Poems are thoughtforms cadenced to lyricism. Shashaani also peppers the book with declarative statements, integrated within the pages.

If we ask what voice the poet uses throughout this book, it appears as if she has forgotten her own to find a supreme voice. She

makes a prayer for all the children in the distance. In *"Oneness,"*
Avideh Shashaani says:

The silence of the desert
allows each leaf,
each moment be heard with
a clarity that lets us release
the boundaries we've drawn
between ourselves and existence.

...

Each poem in this volume is different in nature. Each wants to
frame reality in a new way, but together, they form the divine
search for love. Out of the documentaries of despair, Shashaani
calls for what is dormant in the world but must be awakened in the
reader. From complication and conflict of spirit the author invokes
a vital reckoning of conscience.

Clearly, it is the God Avideh is devoted to that she finds folded in
the immortal wings of poetry, which inspired her to write this book.

_____

Grace Cavalieri
Producer: "The Poet and the Poem from the Library of Congress,"
*   for public radio.*

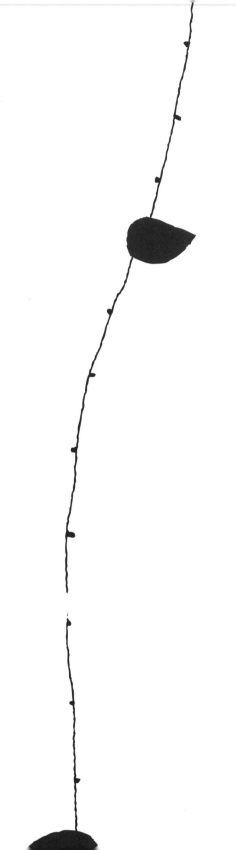

The genocide in Bosnia placed my pulse in the frightened hands of the children of war and I began to hear their plaintive tears through the texture of my skin. Many years have passed since then and we still continue to destroy the verdant hearts of tomorrow. Maybe there's one ray of hope left. Maybe our children's children will see the folly of destruction and life on the planet will resume with the hue of respect for all life.

TELL ME WHERE TO BE BORN

People of the world,
tell me where to be born.

If I were born in the land
of "your interest"
would you let me die?

People of the world,
my name is Holocaust and
I'm fifty plus years old.

My name is Sarajevo and
I'm three years old.

My name is Rwanda and
I'm but a month old.

I have no name,
I'm yet to be born.

People of the world,
tell me where to be born
so you will not hate me one day,
so you will not maim me one day,
so you will not kill me one day.

People of the world,
tell me where to be born.

"I"

I looked in a mirror and saw
a familiar face
we looked at each other
I said, "Who are you?"
"A stranger," she replied
I said, "Where are you from?"
"I have no home," she said
"I'm as ancient as time
and as young as tomorrow
but tell me, who are you?
where did you come from?"
I said, "I'm as young as you
and as old as tomorrow
I'm yet to be born
I have no home."

THE HEARTLAND

Rivers of sorrow always
find a resting place–
in a village,
in a home,
in the eyes
of an abandoned child.

We cannot claim to be civilized as long as our children are exploited and human trafficking takes place.

CHILD SOLDIER

If I were to glide my hand
over the surface of the rough
mountainous terrain
would I know how harshly
the world has treated you?

Would I know how much
you've suffered and the memories
of pain that run through
your withered wings?

I touch the edge
of your soul and see the haunted
look in your vacant eyes telling
me your soul left long ago
when humans used innocence
to murder for their cause.

LEAVE THEM ALONE

O you vile Merchants of children,
my ears began to scream
when I heard you sell infants
of six months to pedophiles
who say, "the younger the better,
can I torture it, kill it?"

You steal innocents from the fields,
from the streets, from the devastated
ruins of war, from the heart of mother
earth and feed them as scraps of meat to these
vampires of children's flesh.

Is there no drop of human blood left
in your veins?

Is there no shame left in the world?

CAN YOU BREATHE

Can you breathe?
My nostrils are numb
from the sharp edges
of the air I can't inhale
the pain—that rides each
molecule of air—
from the sighs of the orphans
abandoned to their fate.

TENDERNESS

This morning my eyes
saw two jasmines bloom
next to each other.

Hold me in your heart
and kiss me.

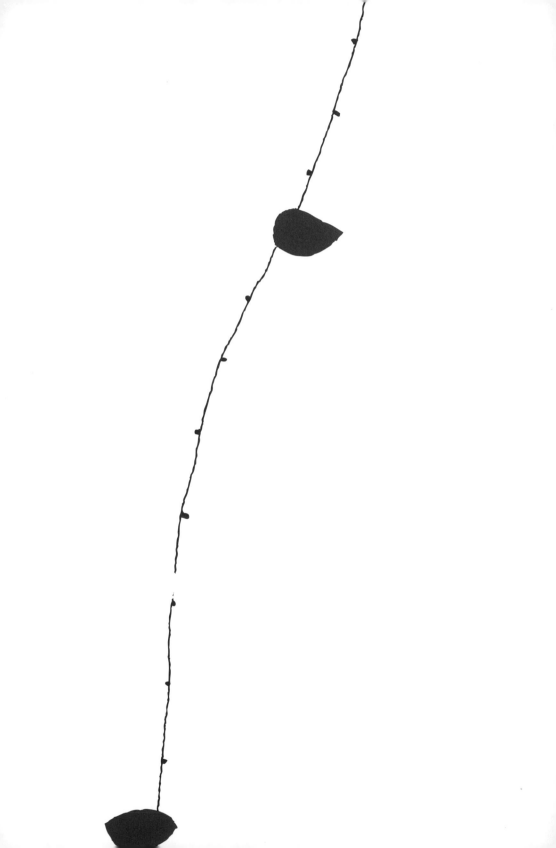

Humans have turned the instinct to survive into a deranged manifestation—hoarding, dominating, and creating temples of self-worship.

KILL ME

O mother, father, God, holy man

I plead with you

kill me before you

abandon me in the streets

kill me before you

push me in the ring of vultures

kill me before you

sell me to the pimps,

the pedophiles, the thieves

kill me before you

let others kill my soul

I plead with you

kill me before they kill my soul.

"MAMA"

On the day of parting you left in silence
and didn't look at me.
I held your hand and you placed
in it a piece of dried bread.
The crowd kept pushing and all
I could see were the bare feet of
fleeing people trapped in the blaze
of fear.

What is your name "mama"?
What is my name "mama"?
How do we find each other
when I don't know your name
or mine?

Knees keep banging against my head
as the crowd pushes and presses.
Feet rush but cannot go far,
it's difficult to breathe.
All I can see are the bare feet of
fleeing people trapped in the blaze
of fear.

BAPTISM POOL

As the days go by

and the nights close in

my heart becomes

a baptism pool

from the plaintive tears

of the children lost to war.

ETERNITY

I live to live

in the moment

between two

moments.

Like fish swimming

between the waves.

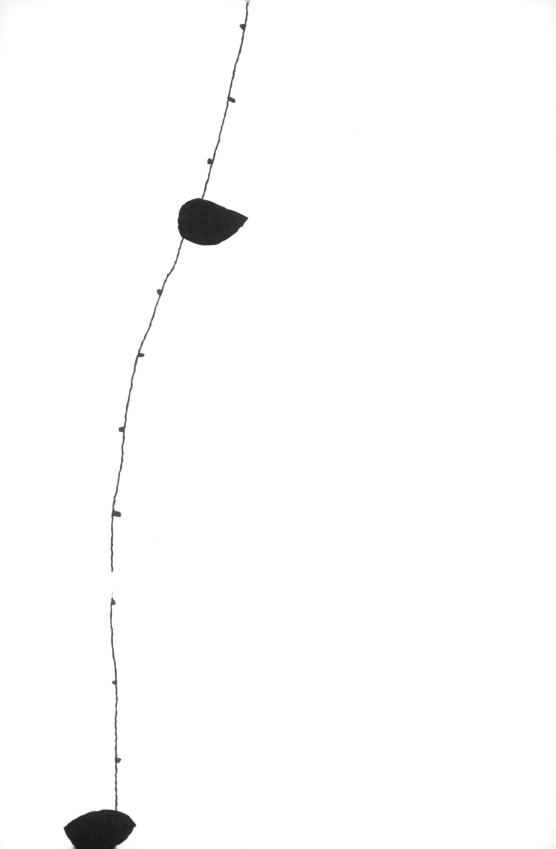

Power doesn't have foresight. If it did, it wouldn't change hands.

ONCE UPON A TIME

Once upon a time I dreamt of true visions,
those were the times when my heart was clear.
Once upon a time I loved,
those were the times when my heart was innocent.
Once upon a time,

Once upon a time I cradled innocence
with lullabies of ancient myths.
Once upon a time I was the womb
where fertility nested.

Once upon a time ceased to be
when humans began to hate
when humans began to kill
when innocence faded from
the edge of the universe.

Once upon a time love was
the touch of tenderness.
Once upon a time there was no
edge to the universe.

Yes, once upon a time ceased
long ago.

But dreamers still have visions
of a universe
without an edge,
and
they cradle their dreams
as lullabies
waiting
to be born in
a universe without an edge.

WHEN THE RIVER RISES

I hear the clamor of tambourines
I hear the wailing of the crowd
I hear the retreating sound of footsteps
I hear the sound of my teardrops
falling from my frozen gaze
I hold her to my breast
hoping she will stir
waiting for her lips
to search for the nipple
she knew so well
the milk had dried days ago
but she hadn't cared
I feel her body getting
colder and colder
my tears running on her
frail body so badly bruised
"Take me, spare my child"
they only laughed as they
forced me to the floor and
flung her against the wall...
I whisper in her soul...
"When the river rises we will
disappear together my child."

njustice ultimately destroys its own agents.

EXILE

You forced us out of
our homes, our land.

You murdered, mutilated,
defiled our men, women, and
children.

We've made new homes on
borrowed land—
in camps, cities, and
borderlands.

You think you've taken
all we had
but we ride the wings of hope
and time is on our side.

The memory of our home,
our land, our people,
grows day by day like the oak
tree that stands up tall and slowly
uproots all that's been built
on the ground.

Hope is a self-sustaining river
that revives dejected hearts
by its lyrical and transcendent strength.

Oppression is fragile, like glass
it shatters at the hands of its own
reckless merchants of war.

TEA LEAVES

My eyelids close and my
eyes follow my fingertips
tracing the invisible
lines in my palm looking
into a future that seems
to have been left behind.

PROMISE

Like the awakened breeze
of an early dawn
untouched by the waves
of human thought

the face of a baby stirs
the promise of hope
in a heart that's seen too much
of how the world works.

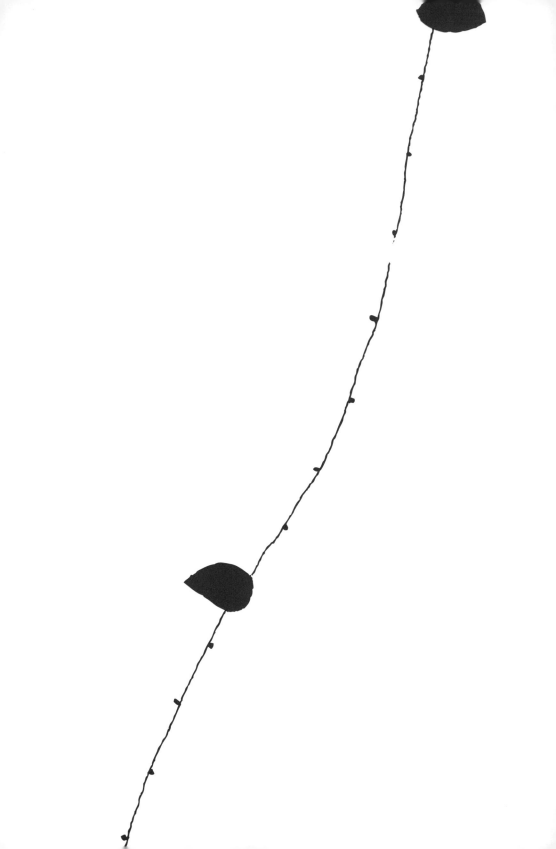

When we put aside our self-interest, we can stand up for truth.

DARFUR

I see the thunder of our pain
in the mirage of our dreams.
Anguish is kindled into ashes
where the silent owls keep watch
over a people abandoned to despair.

We are pillaged by hunger, disease,
and the carnage of ethnic wars.
Our children are left to care for
each other, to fend for themselves.
They're sold in traffic and lured
by the mercenaries of war!

It's always autumn here.
People falling by the wayside
being blown away by death
like autumn leaves decomposing
on the earth.

We have no ruby mines, diamond mines,
we have no oil fields.

The world looks elsewhere as we
fall by the wayside as autumn leaves
slowly decomposing on the earth.

The world looks elsewhere—
we have nothing they can take
from us!

IN THE SHADOW OF GRIEF

Is it the sound of my
hair growing white
or is it the sound
of your laughter that
clings to my mind,
my child?

Is it the echo of my heartache
that trails in my breath
or is it the sound
of your quivering footsteps
returning home,
my child?

Each night I steal my way
to the celestial spheres, searching
for you in the vast expanse
of the star-filled sky where grief's
dark shadow cannot walk
between us,
my child.

MOMENTS

I remember the times when I cradled you
in my arms, or carried you on my back
when we went from village to village looking
for food and a place to rest.

I remember the times when you sat by my side
while I washed our clothes by the riverside,
while I prepared rice over a dwindling
fire in a field surrounded
by mountains under the summer sky.

How can I go on living if I don't
have your memories to accompany
me each day, my child.

NOW

There are so many flowers
so many trees, pebbles, fish,
stars, and galaxies.

I love to gaze at all
that is
and leave behind a world
ablaze
with uncertainties.

njustice uproots our shared humanity.

SCARLET TEARS

I long to see tomorrow
filled with children's playful songs.
The curtain of today veils the horizon
and the blade of grief penetrates
my heart, and the children become
invisible songs of sorrow.

The taste of sadness doesn't leave
my eyes, and I claw at the veil
that imprisons the hope of the children
of tomorrow.

I begged the world, give
the children a chance, stop exploiting
their innocence, their verdant minds.

We've exploited and destroyed the earth,
there's nothing left for our callous greed to devour.

Where else can we see the face of innocence
if our children become like us?

I begged the world to give the children a
chance.
I journeyed through the night and anguish
became the whisper in my tears.

I split open a pomegranate
and saw the future of the world,
I saw the scarlet tears of children
haunted by the memories of war.

Don't grieve for me now. My soul died
long ago. I begged the world
to leave innocence alone,
but no one listened. All I see now
are the scarlet tears of the children,
the children of war.

ONE MORE TIME

O garden of sorrow!
O Lady of darkness!
Let my child's glance cradle my love
one more time before you take her
on her journey along the mountain-pass

Let her see my eyes
one more time before you take her
on her journey along the mountain-pass

Let me hold her
one more time before you wrap me
in the dark tomb of the forgetful earth
without seeing my child.

It takes wisdom to see the fragility of power.

VULTURES OF GREED

Are you satisfied now?
Are you content?
Look how you've destroyed
so many hopes and lives.
Look beneath the mask
that hides your soul!

I know you can't see.
You breathe the air
that never left the cesspool
of greed.

It's your turn to carry
the torch for the vultures
of greed.

Yes, it's your turn
to silence innocence.
It's your turn to
sacrifice innocence
at the altar of power
where the vultures
infest the skies of hope.

It's almost too late
there's one ray of hope left
before darkness tightens its grip
before innocence is slaughtered
before your soul sinks in the
abyss of no-return.

LOSS

How much of our soul
do we give up to
become powerful
and what must we
give up to regain our
soul.

SALAAM MY CHILDREN

If someone should ask
what of the world saddens your heart
and what of the world brings a smile
I will answer
the suffering I see in the eyes
of an innocent child
and the joyful laughter
of a happy child.

Salaam my children, salaam
to each of you, hurt and turned away
by grown ups like us, neglected and abused
hungry and bruised. O my children
without childhood, suffering and in pain
peace be with you, children of today.

INNOCENCE

When I look at a baby's
hands, feet, unblemished
skin, and see in its eyes
the fullness of life,

I know that I am still
alive and the tree
of hope has survived.

Power slowly corrupts the occupier. Striving for freedom strengthens the occupied.

LOST

I open the windows of my soul to enfold
you in my stillness, to unravel
the cobwebs that have enclosed your soul,
my son.

But all I see is the lust for blood in your eyes
I see no memory in your face that says
you remember you too were once a child.

When did you forget you have a soul? When
did you forget you don't uproot a seed
planted by another's hand?

WILL I KNOW TOMORROW

Sometimes I wonder
what it would be like to be a child.

What does the world look
like through their eyes?

How do men see the world,
women, and themselves?

What would it be like to be
a gazelle, fish, lion, or rose?

What would it be like to be
a mother, grandmother, sister,
all the things I will never know?

The earth gave me birth
but, will I know tomorrow?

LITTLE RAIN DROP

Little raindrop, no one told you
what your fate would be,
no one warned you—
you crashed and shattered
into infinite pieces, your remnants
moving along aimless rivulets.

Mother moon keeps watch over the midnight
sky as father sun prepares
for the forthcoming day, a promise
of faith, a renewal of hope

When all promises fail,
when the sun and moon fade from the sky
and there's no warmth or light, walk
into my heart, little tiny raindrop,
and rest.

Striving for excellence is a sign of intelligence. Striving for power is a sign of an unlived heart.

IMPRINT

Nothing can leave the universe:
after all, where can it go?
We go to war,
we kill, we destroy,
we mutilate, we plunder
the people, the land.

When will we realize
the agonized cries
of those we've sentenced to death
find their way into
the collective unconscious
of all of us day to day,
generation after generation,
someone must pay...
Nothing leaves the universe: after all,
where can it go?

TOMORROW

We lift our eyes to see the sky, to escape
the fires of sorrow but the sky is covered with veils
of sadness, for our souls died long ago
when the mirror of innocence became covered
with the scarlet tears of the children of war.

MOTHER EARTH

I touch the soul of the earth,
feel the sigh of despair move
through my fingertips.

I am all you have,
I am your home,
I am your life,
I've given you all
I have.

Look what you've done to me
look what you're doing
to each other.

HERITAGE

Beneath the smooth surface
of your words are the murderous
chants that blindfold ignorant minds
to exploit, murder, rape, torture,
to carry out your acts of vengeance, all
in the name of God!

BOUNDARIES

You say,

your God is better than mine.

You say,

your God is mightier than mine.

You say,

your God is loving, kind, forgiving.

I say,

no one has a monopoly on God,

if God is God.

The tide of pain washes away what is inconsequential from one's heart.

TSUNAMI

The heaven of sorrow

spreads over an endless trail

where the glaciers have frozen

in time the frightened cries of the villagers

who never had a chance

to withstand the thrust of nature's fury.

A narrow pulse quietly moves her eyelid open.

My children,

I wish I could place each one of you

one by one

as tender petals around my heart

and enclose you in my embrace

under a glass dome untouched

by nature's fury.

Can I rest in the shadow of a vague dream?

Sorrow swiftly rushes its burning

grip and I awake from the slumber

of a vague dream and see you

before my eyes swallowed

by a vicious sea.

RECKLESS

In the wake of a mid-winter night the revelers
flung the flames of lust on the azure
waters of the Andaman Sea as the dust
of death rose from the sweltering waves
making their way to every home, shelter, place
of refuge.

OFFERING

O my tears of sorrow
I offer you to the south winds
to you O gods of vengeance
I offer my last remnants of ruin
to you summer of life
I offer the harvest of my youth
freedom's sanctuary neatly
embroiders its cradle
in shades of ivory silk
the north winds are drawn
into the sunrise where
the bosom of life is to unfold
a new leaf upon the tree of hope.

DIARY

In the lines of the curving sand

I draw my dreams

knowing that with each tide

I can draw new ones

in the lines of the curving sand.

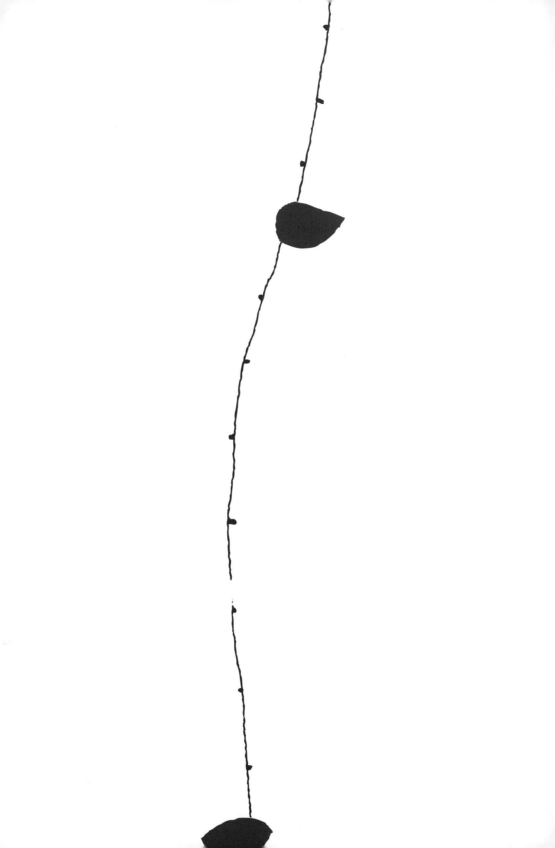

There is no boundary in the universe. Life in all its aspects is an invisible spectrum forever evolving.

ABIQUIU

The desert lays bare
its breasts without a hint
of shame under the turquoise
dome of the sky,
exposing its naked truth
to all passersby.

NATURE

There is no friction
between the flower
and the bee.

The flower and
the bee know
survival
depends on one another.

A RECOLLECTION

When I walk along a dusty trail the pebbles
navigate their way in the form of images
I recognize in the labyrinth of my heart.

I bend down and pick each one up and feel
their warmth in the palm of my hand. I bring
them home and string them one

by one on a golden thread as an invisible
memory around my heart.

YOUTH

The translucency of a dewdrop
on the tender petals of a new bloom
reminds me of a time when I had
no fears—a time when the vigor of youth
laid no claim on the past nor
on the future.

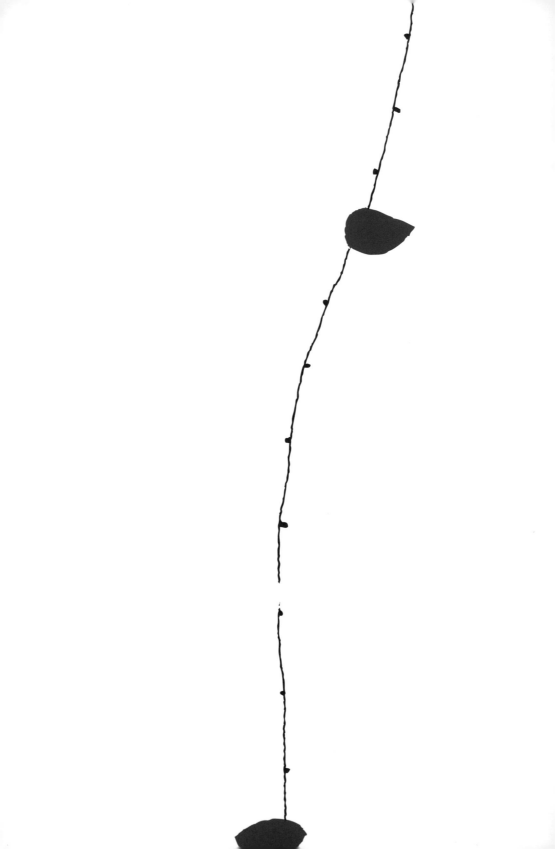

Sadness and innocence are the two faces of my soul. Sadness is the reflection of total wisdom when it sees innocence enter the realm of substance. Wherever innocence goes sadness moves in its shadow. When innocence is in total alignment with wisdom, sadness no longer exists.

TAKE MY ASHES

O people of heart

listen to my distress

I journeyed through the dark

I passed through the blazing fire

I left the ruins behind

the oceans have called me

O people of heart

I have brought you my ashes

let me smell the earth

one more time

let the earth take my tears

and in return grow vineyards

O people of heart

remember me when you

drink of the vineyard's wine

remember the traveler who

brought you her ashes

and in their place vineyards grew

O people of heart

drink and remember me

let the oceans take my ashes

let the waves sway me to and fro

deeper and deeper into the horizon

until I forget this journey of darkness.

66

WALL OF INNOCENCE

Build a wall of innocence
whispers at daybreak
eclipse in my heart
the train of your smile
moments of fragile longing

When day parted
I mourned for a
concealed dream that
would never return.

Cups of memories
set before the sun
sinking into the sand
streaming through pebbles
the wild poppies covering
the hills with their scarlet hue
speak of a concealed dream
that lay bare before the sun.

CIVILIZATION

We don't see stones rushing
to gather around
to be together,
we don't see flowers,
plants or trees
doing the same,
but when we move up the ladder
we do see
birds flock together,
ants trail after one another,
cows and sheep
come together
but they don't hurt each other
for no reason.

Humans come together,
they hurt, and hurt,
there's incest, abuse,
torture and rape;
there's so much hurt.

What will it take for violence to end,
so humans cease to hurt and be hurt?

ALCHEMY

One day when I was distraught
by how violence had penetrated
our world, I remembered

The words of the wisest man who ever lived—
"Wherever there's illness the remedy is next to it."

Think how these words could apply
to healing our planet. Remember the ancients remedy.

Alchemy—transforming base metals
into pure gold. The secret of alchemy—

harness our base instincts that drive the ego to extremes,
nurture the soul with tenderness, beauty, and love

The more the soul is engaged, the less the ego
has a chance to go astray.

Ego and soul were born side by side.
Our will is what keeps the balance between
darkness and light.

Our strength of will is like a single match
that can set a whole forest on fire.

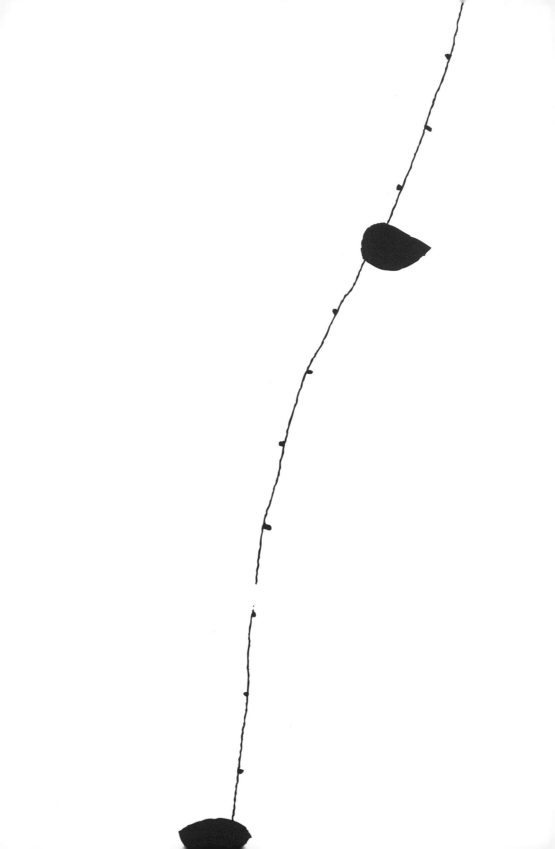

Why should we be colorblind when nature flaunts its colors! Each entity in creation lends its shape, color, and texture to make the canvas of nature so magnificent.

WHAT SETS US APART

You say you have more money,
more education, more power,
and this sets us apart.
Don't you see, all of us—
no matter how rich or poor—
eat, excrete, inhale, exhale....
share the same vital functions.

Besides look at the billions of years
of our shared cosmic past.
How can eighty some years on the planet
determine who has precedence
over the other?
Nothing but our humanity
matters at the end.

ONENESS

The silence of the desert
allows each bird, each leaf,
each moment to be heard with
a clarity that releases
the boundaries we've drawn between
ourselves and existence.

Perhaps, this is why people of the desert
hear the call of God without effort.

SURVIVE

We work and toil

whether rich or poor,

lowly or powerful.

The rich and powerful work

to keep, to increase what they have.

the poor and lowly toil

to survive, perhaps to become

rich and powerful.

To survive we must understand the reason for all

the plunders and massacres brought about

by human hands, celebrated

as victories and conquests by people throughout time.

To truly survive we must discover

our human dignity,

learn to see the uniqueness

of all life.

Defining ourselves by boundaries is denying the interdependence of all that exists.

ARROGANCE

We are invisible in your eyes.

What could you do without us?

We harvest, process, deliver
the food you eat.
We build the homes
you live in, clean them,
wash your cars,
collect your garbage.

We take care of your kids,
your tennis courts, golf courses . . .
is there anything in your lives
that doesn't have the remnant of us
left on it?

TO BE

Each entity in nature
is true to its essence.

A tree doesn't strive
to be a river,
a bird doesn't roar
like a lion.

And yet, to survive,
nature shows
immense flexibility.

Nature evolves by necessity
not by whim.

UNFALTERING STRENGTH

When I look at a slender leaf
of grass or the tender stem
of the lily of the valley
I wonder
how this fragile life pushed
its way through the harsh
dense earth.

Was it difficult, was it painful,
or was the urge to survive
and push out of the darkness
of the earth so great that nothing
else mattered?

A QUESTION

If wisdom means that we have learned
from our experiences, I wonder

if wisdom makes us cautious, prevents us
from embarking on new adventures.

A REMINDER

No two generations have
been alike. It's pointless

to expect our children to benefit
from our experiences. Each generation excavates

its own resources to deal
with the changing environment. This
is evolution in progress.

The world is a symphony and each one of us is an instrument whose music must be played to its utmost magnificence. Even sorrow has its own unique tune.

UNNAMED

You are all I have.
Through you I become
wind without a memory
and wrap myself around
each slender swaying
branch and leaf of the willow tree
make my way through the oceans,
the desert, the jagged edges
of mountaintops.

Through you I become
the honeybee reaching
for the nectar of the honeysuckle
or the honeysuckle waiting
for the humming visits
of the honeybee.

Like a whistle that sets out and becomes
invisible, through you I become
anything I desire.

How can I not be free
if I still have you?
No one can take you from me.

You are all I have.
You are what takes me out
of the bounds of this penitentiary.

PASSAGEWAY

We seek a passageway
away from the imprint of time
where we can rest and move
away from the insecurities of time
secure to know that we no longer
need to toil to keep
the child within intact.

FATE

Perhaps we can look at life as a series
of crossroads. At some we stop but
move on. At others we change
direction. But at one special place—
our sacred space—
we remain.

Who is to say we should
have taken one road over another

if we have arrived at our sacred place.

PERSIA

The shadow of the moon whispered its
lament in a hushed veil over the scented
pastures where the wild deer journeyed
along the hyacinth shaded meadows leaving
a trail of raw musk behind.

The poet's words mingled with the fragrance
of the night blooming jasmine and the lovers
became invisible under the shade of the
weeping willow tree.

The perfume of desire spread through the air
and the nightingale summoned its sonorous
love-songs for the rose.

The night pulls back its skirt and unlocks its
jewels from the vault of the sky and once again
we leave the day at the gate and leaf through
the pages of an ancient past too glorious to
be left behind.

Love is not patient. Its fire expands and consumes. Sadness is patient. Brick by brick it lays its foundation.

A VEILED FACE

The moisture of her eyes
flowed as an endless river
through sandy tracts whose thirst
is never quenched.

Ease my sorrow, unravel
the serpent's grip from my garment
of innocence.

Let my tears of death
put to rest the ruined dwellings
of darkness
with their blush of shame.

YESTERDAY

I keep peeling the robes of darkness
from the fragrant face of dawn
but all I see are the silhouettes of marble
statues that once carried life's enduring
pulse to our fingertips.

I told you, jealousy is a yellow
liquid that slowly turns to orange,
becomes flaming red and finally
destroys the heart.

Now, decked in memory's garb you look
for the rising moon that eclipses the face
of our fragrant dawn.

WILL YOU WEEP WITH ME

Will you weep with me when I weep inside
you? O ache of my heart—
where the full moon of darkness has set
where the musk no longer sings
where my songs have lost their scarlet blush.
Where are the verdant meadows
that brought news of nocturnal visits?
Where are the promised visions of ecstasy
with which my heart conversed?
Where are the flames of longing
that betrayed my rapturous love?
Where is that wine of intimacy
that once embraced my soul?
Will you weep with me when I weep
inside you?

I said to the wind, will you touch
my heart again? I begged the fire,
I prostrated myself before the sun,
the new moon and the stars:
has the universe collapsed?
Can't anyone hear me?
Shall I weep alone?

The sun closes its doors.
The moon splits and breaks into shadows.
The stars converge and form a crescent
in remembrance of days, where shadows were not born.

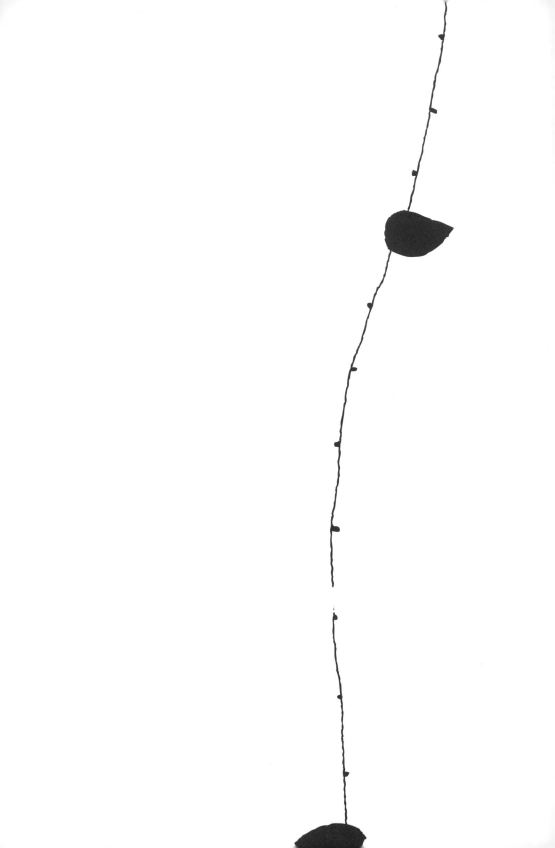

Expecting earthly love to be eternal is like tying stones to the wings of a butterfly.

TIME

I restlessly pushed myself
out of your heart
you reached for the heart
you had lost, but I
saw a face forgotten behind
a mirror stained with rust.

PATIENCE

My eyes became the tilled land,
the meadow, the river,
the past you left behind.
I bathed my soul in the drowned tears
of a life fragmented with sorrow

. . . . .

I feel the pastures of my heart
bursting with the first signs
of spring, the colors
of the moon, of sky,
of rainbow, that never fade.

IMMORTALITY

I've placed my life in color-coded

cubes of time, wrapped each

in a cocoon where butterflies

become butterflies and escape

the chronicles of time.

DON'T THINK

To be in love with love
is the music of my soul.

Don't think about what will happen.

Don't worry if it will last.

Just be in love with love
and it will always be
yours.

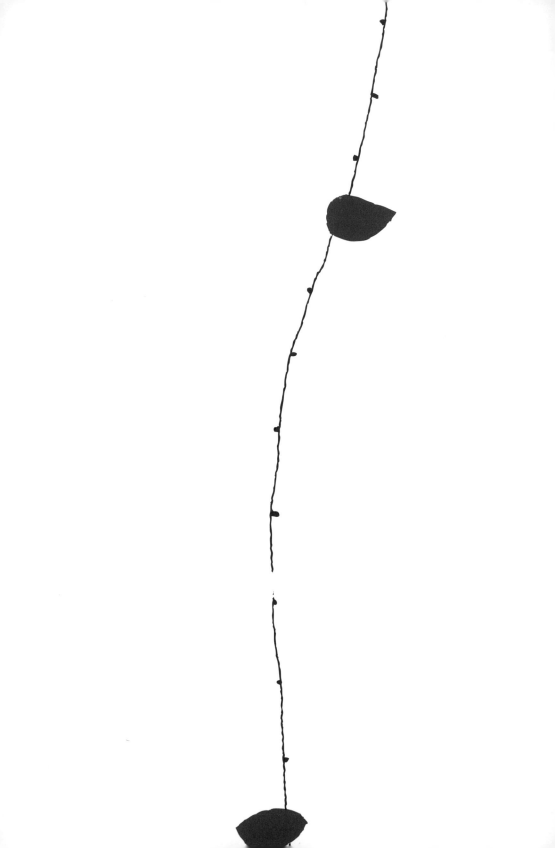

We are all apt to make mistakes. If God is so forgiving, why are we so unforgiving?

A NEW DAY

In the middle of the rubble
where my soul lived in exile,
I found my heart.

YOU AND I

If you haven't suffered
as much as I have
how can you know
the state of my heart?

If you haven't given
your heart to love
how can you lay claim
to God?

If our paths are to converge
you must let go
of fear and embrace
the suffering that comes
with living with love.

RHAPSODY

You are the master musician
and I am the instrument
in your hand that drives us
to ecstasy in a silence
that only our eyes
understand.

The search for God leads us to our self and in finding our self we discover God.

ENCOUNTER

We met

and I saw myself in your eyes

we talked

and my soul awakened

we loved

and I felt the oneness of being.

You closed your eyes to the world

and my universe collapsed.

Many years have passed

there's still a special place

in my heart for you.

You were the mirror

in which I first saw myself.

With each new encounter

a flower blooms in my heart and unfolds

a hidden song of my soul.

That's how I've come to know
the only way to hear one's own song
is to open the door of the soul
and become a mirror
for others to see their souls.

The rivulets of love move
through my heart and veins
celebrating the mysteries
of my own soul.

Now I know what love is—it's the reflection
of one's own self in the mirror
of the world. Emanuel Kant said
beauty does not show us the state
of the external world, instead,
it shows us the beauty
within our own souls.

A NEW MOMENT

When, at the cusp of bewilderment
and amazement, as love
and longing merge, tears
of thankfulness stream
through my heart, slowly
bringing to resonance the whispers
my ears had long waited to hear.

SALZBURG

We entered a city that showcased the best it had
of its historic past and it reminded
us of a small paradise.

We entered our place of sojourn
and that too was a small paradise.

We came together the first day
and someone said,
My name means paradise.

We lived together and shared our hearts,
our work, our thoughts, our visions for tomorrow.

As we talked it became so very clear,
each one of us had a vision of transforming
the world into a paradise.

I realized then that if we can envision paradise
it must be that our hearts are adorned
with the beauties of paradise.

The day came we had to return
to our native lands and share the beauties
of our hearts with a world
in hunger for paradise.

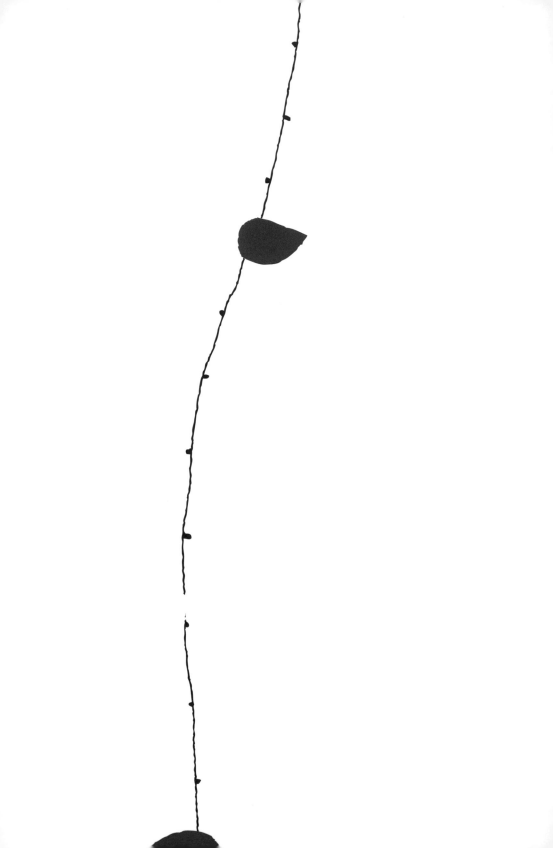

We are a never-ending journey.

SECRET CHAMBER

Each one of us held a key
that unlocked a secret
chamber in the other's heart

As we came together we
realized that we were
the hidden part
of each other's soul

Like an illumined candle
placed at the center
of a mirrored chamber
hidden from the world

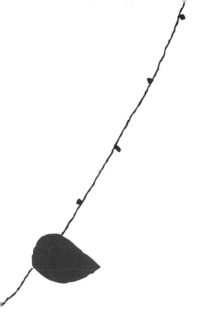

We became the candle
whose reflection is seen
in uncounted ways
in the mirrored chamber
hidden from the world

As we stood side by side
in a circle
of unbroken light

We unlocked, one by one,
all the chambers
that remained locked
in each other's heart.

TRANSCENDENCE

You may worship Me
as a statue, as nature,
or a fixture in your
imagination.

You admonish Me
whenever something
goes wrong in your lives.

And you see yourselves
as the masters of all the
good that comes your way.

If you transcend
the limitations
you've set for yourselves,
you will know there is
no boundary between
your will and Mine.

If you take your "self"
out of the equation,
you will see that you
are no other than
"I".

Haven't I said, "I am
closer to you
than your jugular vein."?

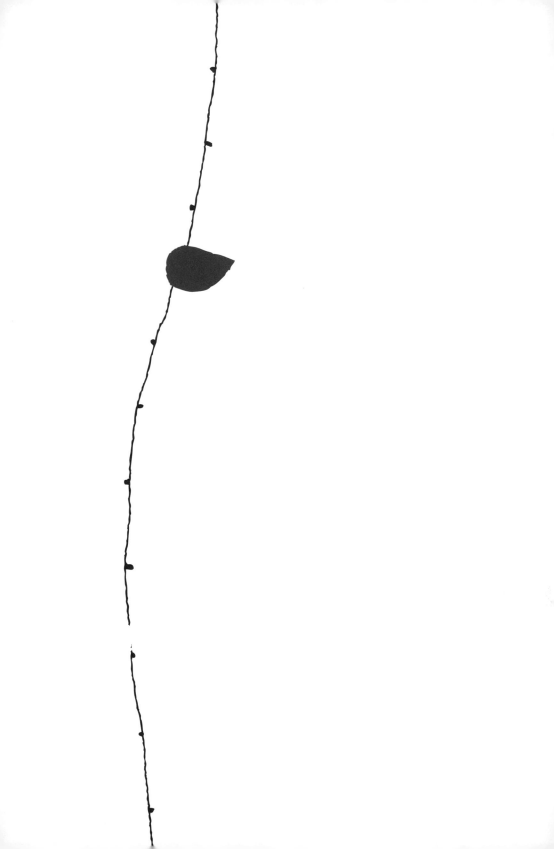

The only relationship that no other human being

can judge is our relationship with God.

NOTHING TO GIVE

I ride the wings of love.
there is nowhere else to be
there is nothing anyone
can take from me
that I will not willingly give.

There is nothing I have
that is mine
I gave up all when
I stood naked before God
and asked to be loved.

VISITATION

There's a festival
awakening in my pulse
as the night draws its curtain
and the sounds of distant bells
speak of a visitation
to take place, a pilgrimage
to the center of being
an incessant merging
of darkness and light
a silent motion from
one to the other
a vacillating heartbeat
too frail to submit.

LOVE

There's a time before sunrise
and a time before sunset
when the horizon and the earth disappear
one into the other
remaining as a single thread of mist.

These are the moments when the longing
in my heart is the greatest
for you, my beloved.

BELOVED

How shall I thank you—
for sparking into fumes
the rust from my veins
tell me, how shall I thank you
shall I kiss your eyes, your face,
your lips, shower you with kisses
of ecstasy over and over
and over again shall I
ask the winds to summon
from the land of nightingales all the roses
that ever bloomed and enclose you
in an embrace of rarefied rose petals
shall I call upon the gods to send forth
their chariots of gold
take you on a journey of never
ending dreams shall I beseech
the mother of all pearls to bed
the rarest crimson pearls and offer them
as my heart's joy, tell me,
how shall I thank you?

SUBMISSION

I inhale the breath of God
through my heart.

Like a reckless whirlwind
I whirl and whirl
in a spin of selfless
ecstasy pushing through
the chambers of the heart
until the heavens open
their gates and invite me
into your embrace, my beloved God.

COME WITH ME

I opened the secret chamber
of rapture and invited you
in.

I said, come fly with me
and dance the dance
of ecstasy.

You backed away
afraid to leave
all you have behind.

I can't wait.

I must go now
the door
is about to close
I must dance
the dance of ecstasy
my beloved
is calling me.

TALISMAN

Is it you that I adore
or are you a filament
of my imagination
come to life?

Is it you that brought
my heart to life,
or is it a long awaited
dream realized?

Each night I place
my languishing heart
in the palm of my eyes
hoping it will venture
out beyond the horizon
where dreams leave
the world behind.

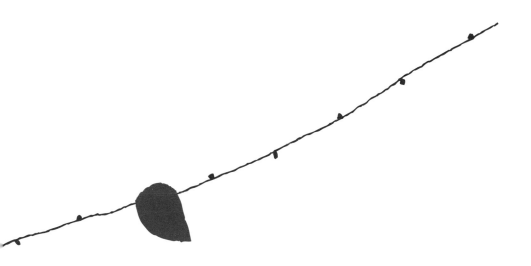

Each morn when I awake
from a wakeful slumber
my eyes in a drunken
swoon caress your
memory over and over
and over
again.

Is it you that my heart
races towards, or is it
a rarefied dream
enclosing me in its embrace?

MIDNIGHT SKY

I trace through the midnight sky
the wanderings of my soul
towards you, my beloved God.

Each dawn I awake to the fragrance
that seamlessly steals its way
through the invisible slumber
that subdues my prayerful heart.

And I know that the wings of time
once again will ring the bells
that take my soul through
the labyrinth of the world.

But, I don't mind.
My soul knows that
once again I shall trace
through the midnight sky
the wanderings of my soul
towards you, my beloved God.

Each reality is rooted in hope and each hope is anchored in a reality beyond our human existence.

FAIRY TALES

I often wonder why little children love fairy tales,
and why grown-ups cease to believe in them.

When children are born
their souls are clear and pure—
unhampered by earthly inputs,
they're totally connected
and behold events from the soul's clear eye.

As we grow and grow
and the world takes hold,
the messages of the soul cease
to reach the heart and we lose
touch with our true home, where goodness
love, and tenderness prevail
and everything seems like a fairy tale.

In fairy tales, the story always ends well.
Grown-up kids can make the connection with the land
of fairy tales again.

And once the connection's made, the heart's door
is unlocked and we live in a state called heaven
on earth—known to children as the land
of fairy tales.

Fairy tales are true,
children see them in dreams,
it's when we grow up
they become tales.

DESTINED

Stars align and continents merge,
the sun folds the night away and impregnates
the dawn sky with its primordial light.

The sky brims with pride unveiling
its turquoise dome and boundless grace
prepares the earths to receive
its blessed child.

Eyes fixed, the eagle pierces deeply
into the horizon.

Vision weds destiny.

The eagle spreads its wings
and raindrops settle on the mouth
of the accepting earth.

Hope steps out of fear's golden cage.

Doves are set free and dust-clouds lift
the ashes of yesterday from the chambers
of tomorrow.

Truth Speaks.

Destiny guides the "Eloquent Word."

Unburdened hearts recognize the song
of truth. A tidal wave toward
something beyond us draws
us closer and closer. There's a shift
in the silence of the heart, intuition
is awakened.

New seeds burst with vitality.

The voice of unity redeems
a youthful nation's history, woven
in its shameful shades of past.

The call beckons all to a sacred place,
rivers run parallel, rushing to join
the sea.

The triumphant song of hope echoes
through the vastness of the skies,
and the vision of a "Dream" secures
its long-awaited destiny.

ANGELINA

There is a place called Harbor
of Hope and within is an intimate
meeting place called Island
of Faith secured by the Anchorage
of Belief and adorned with the courage
to hope, the faith to trust,
and belief to share.

Here, children of tomorrow are reared
in the bosom of radiance,
their lyrical bodies dipped
in the pool of wisdom scented
with the hues of sweet innocence, the halo
of enchantment, the fragrance of love.

Here, my precious one,
I will rear you and nurture you.

Here, my child, no one can hurt you,
no one will hurt you.

Here, in my bosom…
a place.

I KNOCK ON EVERY DOOR
I BEG THE EARTH AND THE SKY
PLEASE DON'T LET INNOCENCE DIE.

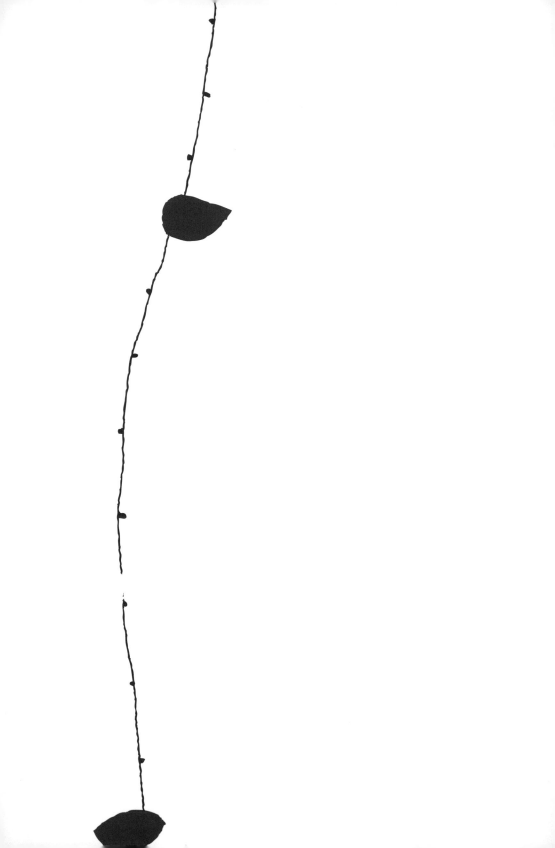